Rhodes

Designed by N. Eliopoulos

Photography by A. Spyropoulos

Distributed by
P. Efstathiadis & Sons S.A.
Athens, 14 Valtetsiou St. Tel. 3615011, 3638680
Thessalonika, 34 Olympou-Diikitiriou St. Tel. 511781

EFSTATHIADIS GROUP
14 Valtetsiou St. - Athens - Tel. 3615011

Nikos Alexis

Rhodes

EFSTATHIADIS GROUP

Introduction

Rhodes, the beautiful, diamond-shaped island, covers an area of 1,400 square km., and is the biggest of all the twelve islands of the Dodecanese. It is 77 kilometres long and 38 kms. wide. Towards the central and western part of the island, Mt. Atavyria, which is surrounded by a range of hills, has its loftiest peak at a height of 1,215 metres. Most of the island's land is very fertile and rich in vegetation. Oranges, lemons, figs, peaches, plums, as well as olives, are to be found in abundance. It isn't at all by chance that Rhodes should be universally known as the "Island of Roses".

Its climate has much in common with that of Eastern Sicily. Temperatures vary between about 10°C in the winter, and 30-32°C in the summer. The island is often swept by strong winds; however, the eastern coastline is more than sufficiently protected. Windmills, which add a picturesque touch to the scenery, turn to advantage the power of the winds. Between April and October the climate tends to be dry, and wet between November and March. The best months to visit the island are April and May, as well as September and October. From springtime until autumn, the island is so inundated by tourists, that one has to book a hotel a long time in advance to make sure there will be no problems because of possible lack of accommodation.

In 1971, the island's population was 66,170, but, owing to tourism, which transformed the island and boosted its economy, the city of Rhodes is developing fast; nevertheless, part of the population is still cultivating the land or breeding animals. The main products are wine, olive oil, tobacco, vegetables, and fruit. Since grazing-land covers one-third of the island, stock-raising (goats, sheep, cattle) is quite developed; another third is covered by forests, a magnificent view of which we can see at Mt. Profitis Elias (Prophet Elijah), its peak and slopes hardly discernible under the dense, evergreen blanket of pine, oak, and cypress trees. At the foot of the mountain, clouds of colourful butterflies complete the matchless beauty of the valley, which was named after this rare phenomenon and is a constant pole of attraction for local and foreign visitors.

4. The Entrance to the Harbour (Mandraki) with the famous bronze Deer.

6. City of Rhodes with beaches on the West Coast.

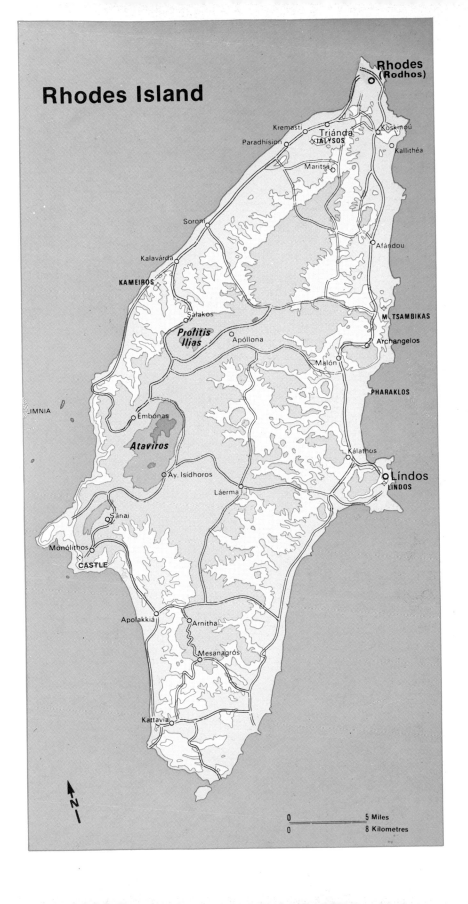

Rhodes Island

Rhodes
(Rodhos)

Kremasti
Paradhision
Triánda
IALYSOS
Koskinoú
Kallithéa

Maritsá

Soroni

Afándou

Kalavárda

KAMEIROS

Sálakos

M. TSAMBIKAS

Profítis
Ilías
Apóllona
Archangelos

Malón

PHARAKLOS

LIMNIA

Embónas

Atáviros

Kálathos

Áy. Isidhoros

Líndos
LÍNDOS

Láerma

Sáṇai

Monólithos
CASTLE

Apolakkiá
Arnitha

Mesanagrós

Kattavia

N

| 0 | | 5 Miles |
| 0 | | 8 Kilometres |

Myth and history
Ancient Rhodes

In ancient times, the island, because of its abundant snakes, was called **Aethrea Ophioussa** (in ancient Greek, óphis = snake); it was also called **Telhinis.** The island of Rhodes has probably taken its name from the Greek word **'rhodon'**, which means rose ... In one of his Odes, **Pindar** talks about the birth of the island, saying that it was the fruit of the union between the sun-god Helios and the nymph Rhoda. In prehistoric times, the island's culture was influenced by that of Crete, and later of Mycenae. Homer mentions three cities of Rhodes, **Lindos, Ialyssos,** and **Camiros** (Iliad II, 656). Those three cities, together with **Kos, Knidos,** and **Alikarnassos,** composed the Dorians' hexapolis (a union of six cities).

Classical and Hellenistic period

Lindos, Ialyssos and Camiros were very prosperous; they extended their commercial activities throughout the Mediterranean, colonized many of the neighboring islands, and even founded colonies along the coasts of Asia Minor and Europe. In the 6th century B.C., they were governed by tyrants. During the wars against the Medes, the people of ancient Media, a kingdom in what is now northwestern Persia, the Rhodians surrendered in 490 B.C., 478 B.C. and in 411 B.C., when they joined the **Alliance of Delos,** as allies-citizens of the state of Athens; in that same year, and while the Peloponnesian War was well under way, they took up arms against the Athenians in order to help the Spartans. In 408 B.C., the three cities united, establishing the City of Rhodes, which they colonized with citizens of their own.

The plans of the new City were made by **Hippodamos,** the most famous architect of that era.

The City of Rhodes, whose architectural layout was much praised by Stravon, began to grow at once; in the beginning it was ruled by an oligarchic government, and in 396 B.C. it was brought under the control of Sparta.

9. *The City of Rhodes besieged by the Turkish army in 1480. Bibliothèque Nationale, Paris.*

10-11. *The City of Rhodes during the first quarter of 16th century.*

Later on, its citizens got a democratic constitution and found themselves in alliance with the Athenians, who, after negotiations with the Persian fleet, helped them to win a victory over the Spartans in the battle of Knidos (394 B.C.). In 378, Rhodes joined the 2nd Confederacy of Athens, but again, in 357 B.C., they rose against the Athenians, having secured the help of the King of Karia, who supplied the city with a garrison. Owing to the fact that, for a while, they were in alliance with the Persians, the Rhodians didn't deny their help to the city of Tyre, when it was besieged by **Alexander the Great.** In 332, they were forced into accepting a Macedonian garrison, but it was done away with soon after the death of Alexander the Great. In the wars that followed, they became allied to **Ptolemy I,** who, in 305 B.C., gave them asssistance, when Demetrios the Besieger laid siege to the city. One year later, Demetrios had to discontinue beleaguering it; his army was in full retreat, abandoning all his heavy weapons. The Rhodians had won another victory. They sold Demetrios' siege machines and used the money they got to set up the famous **Colossus** of Rhodes. They were so grateful to Ptolemy I, the Soter, as they called him (a word of Greek origin, meaning saviour), that they honoured him as if he were a god.

12. *Sunrise: The Mole of Aghios Nikolaos with the three windmills in the background.*

Very soon after the end of the siege by Demetrios, Rhodes reached its zenith of wealth and prosperity. Its harbour became the center of trade between Italy, Greece and Macedonia, as well as Asia and Africa. Its commercial and military fleets made the city the biggest naval power in the Aegean Sea. Its currency and maritime law, the first ever constituted, were respected all over the world. Augustus used it as a model and Justinian followed his example. With a population of 60-80,000 inhabitants, the city was strongly fortified and richly ornamented, and this epoch is considered the beginning of its artistic golden century. Rhodes even managed to derive financial and artistic advantage from the destructive earthquake of 222 B.C., as many states of the ancient world rushed to its assistance. At the end of the first century A.D., even though the city had been plundered of most of its treasures, **Pliny** counted no less than 2,000 statues, many of which were of colossal dimensions. The Rhodians had a great admiration for athletics, music, and rhetoric; Aeschines (389-314 B.C.), having met with complete failure in his attempt to complete with Demosthenes, founded in Rhodes a school of rhetoric, which flourished, turning later into a meeting-place for many distinguished Romans, such as **Cato, Cicero, Julius Caesar,** and

14. *Colossus of Rhodes.*

the poet Apollonius (222-181 B.C.), who was born in Alexandria, lived in Rhodes, and was so successful in his teaching of rhetoric that he was honoured with official recognition and was renowned ever after as Apollonius of Rhodes.

During the 2nd century B.C., the Rhodians concluded an alliance with the Romans, and their help against Philip V of Macedon resulted in the latter's defeat at the battle of Cynocephali in 197 B.C., after which the Cyclades islands were ceded to the Rhodians. As a result of their cooperation with the Romans in the war against Antiochus III, king of Syria, the island extended its influence and territory over a large part of the Syrian colonies of Southern Karia (188 B.C.). Later on, the favourable attitude adopted by Rhodes towards Perseus, the last king of Macedon, resulted in Rome's retaliation, and Rhodes was forced to hand over its colonies in Asia Minor, when Perseus was defeated at Pydna. When Mithridates, king of Pontus, was defeated repeatedly in his wars against the Romans, Rhodes came again under Rome's favour. In the end, Syllas returned to Rhodes all its lost Asiatic colonies. During the Roman civil war, Rhodes fought on the side of Julius Caesar; after he was murdered, Cassius pillaged the city in 43 B.C., seizing a part of the Rhodian fleet and destroying the rest of it. This was a fatal blow for the Rhodian navy.

Roman period

Augustus, though, treated Rhodes well, granting it the title of an Allied State. Vespasian (emperor from 70 until 79 A.D.) made it a province of the Roman Empire, and during the reign of Diocletian, Rhodes became the 'Metropolis' of the province of the islands. During his second or third journey (Acts of the Apostles, XXI, 1), St. Paul visited the island, which soon had its own bishop. During the 4th century A.D., the 'Metropolis' of the islands had a number of bishops under its jurisdiction, and in the 9th century A.D., the Church of Rhodes became independent, no longer under the authority of the Church of Rome. Nonetheless, in 1274, the Metropolitan of Rhodes was present at the Synod of Lyons, and signed his agreement to the ephemeral union of the Eastern and the Catholic Churches.

After the division of the Roman Empire in A.D. 395, Rhodes naturally became a part of the Eastern Empire, and shared its fate. After A.D. 654, it was often raided, and captured for a number of years by the Saracens. In 1082, Byzantium granted the Venetians commercial privileges on the island, and the Crusaders, on their way to the Holy Lands, often stopped at its ports to rest and procure provisions. During the 4th Crusade, after Constantinople had been captured by the Franks, the governor of Rhodes, Leon Gavalas, declared the island independent. Later, the Genoans took control of Rhodes, and in 1306, welcomed the Knights of St. John as refugees. Very soon, they became masters of the island.

Period of the Knights. – Turkish period

The Knights of St. John of Jerusalem, renamed the Knights of Rhodes and later the Knights of Malta, originally had charitable aims; the Order of the Knights of St. John, founded in 1048, soon acquired a military character, and its main objective was to defend the Holy Sepulcher. In 1306, they left Cyprus and settled in Rhodes. In 1309, having repeatedly asked the Emperor to cede them the fief of Rhodes, they took it by force, following a siege of nearly two years.

FOULQUES DE VILLARET 1310 1319
HELION DE VILLENEUVE 1319 1346
DIEUDONNÉ DE GOZON 1346 1353
PIERRE DE CORNEILLAN 1354 1355

ROGER DE PINS 1355 1365
RAYMOND BÉRANGER 1365 1374
ROBERT DE JUILLY 1374 1377
FERDINAND D' HÉRÉDIA 1377 1396

PHILLIBERT DE NAILLAC 1396 1421
ANTOINE FLUVIAN 1421 1437
JEAN DE LASTIC 1437 1454
JACQUES DE MILLY 1454 1461

RAYMOND ZACOSTA 1461 1467
G.B. DEGL' ORSINI 1467 1476
PIERRE D' AUBUSSON 1476 1505
AIMERIE D' AMBOISE 1505 1512

GUY DE BLANCEFORT 1512 1513
FABRIZIO DEL CARRETTO 1513 1521
PH. VILLIERS DE L' ISLE ADAM 1521 1522

16. *The knights of St. John founded in the 11th century lived in seven groups according to nationalities or "tongues": English, French, German, Italian, Province, Anvergne, Aragon and Castile.*

16

*17. The Tower of Naillac.
The Gate of St. Paul.*

18-19. The Eastern side of the tower of St. Nicholas, by Gabriel.

The members of the Order of St. John were divided into three classes: the knights, the clerics, and the pages, who followed the knights. In the 12th century A.D., the organization was divided into seven "Tongues": Provence, Auvergne, France, Italy, Spain (which was later divided into Aragon and Castille), England, and Germany. Each territory had its own leader, and the body of the leaders, presided over by the Grand Master (who held office for life), formed the College of the Order. Today's British Order of St. John, which was founded in 1827, can be regarded as a regeneration of the "Tongue" of England.

Having conquered Rhodes, the Knights of St. John built a powerful fleet, which protected the flourishing commercial activities of the island. For two consecutive centuries they fought against the Turks with success. They took part in the capture and later the defence of Izmir by the Christians, they were also part of the military force which besieged the Sultan of Egypt in 1444, and Mohammed II in 1480, when the general of the Cavalry was an Englishman, John Kendall. Finally, in June 1522, Suleiman I, after having taken Beograd, attacked Rhodes with an

expeditionary force of 100,000 men. The Knights numbered only 650; there were also 200 Genoese sailors, 50 Venetians, 400 Cretans and 600 native Rhodians. Pope Adrian VI made an appeal to the Christian Princes to give the Knights assistance, but it was to no avail. The Turks invaded the island, cutting off all passages towards the sea, positioned their troops on the surrounding hillocks and mounds, and from those points of vantage they bombarded the city and its defenders mercilessly. The besieged never ceased repairing the breaks in the walls, but they kept diminishing in number, became exhausted, and traitors managed to get through, circulating among them. In the following winter, the Turks succeeded in making a big breach in the city walls, which proved fatal. The Knights acknowledged their defeat. On January the 1st, 1523, Grand Master **Villier de l'Isle Adan** left the island with 180 survivors; they took refuge at Heraklion, Crete, and later, in 1530, they established themselves in Malta.

After their departure, the churches were turned into mosques. It took the Fathers of the Mission some 136 years

20. *The Entrance to the Harbour.*
A view of Mandraki. The Palace of Grand Master in the background.

21. Hotels Metropolitan and Rhodes Palace and other hotels in the City of Rhodes.

22. The Minaret and Dome of the Mosque of Suleiman.

before they were able to return to the island and take care of the enslaved population. In 1719, the island was placed under the protection of the Apostolic Prefecture of Constantinople. In 1873, French Sisters of the Order of St. Francis of Assisi founded schools, and in 1899, members of the Christian faith established the College of St. John. In 1877, the island became an Apostolic Prefecture.

23. Fountain in the Centre of Ippokratous square: Old town.

Italian period

In 1912, amidst the turmoil of the war against the Turks, the Italians laid siege to Rhodes and captured it.

Very soon, the rest of the twelve islands of the Dodecanese were also seized by Italian troops, with a view to cutting off Turkish communications with Tripoli, Libya, which Italy wanted to add to its chain of colonies. The Italian Occupation lasted until 1943, much longer than the people of Rhodes could have imagined, and led to mass arrests and deportations. In the Treaty of Lausanne (1923), Turkey ceded its rights on the islands to Italy. It must be mentioned, though, that during the Italian Occupation, the Italians improved and extended the road network; they also founded the Museum and the Archaeological Service, and conducted excavations. In 1943, the island was taken over by the Germans, and was finally liberated in the year 1945, by British and Greek commandos. The Dodecanese was officially incorporated into the Greek State on 7th March, 1948.

The art of Rhodes

The first objects of art that were produced on the island date back to the 2nd millenium B.C. and bear the influence of the Cretan and Mycenaean periods. Excavations have brought to light no magnificent palaces, but room-sized tombs have revealed furnishings for the use of the dead, various ancient vessels and pieces of jewellery, as well as weapons. The pottery is yellow and pink, with relief decorations representing marine animals and flowers; some characteristic features of the decorative patterns are of local origin. The feminine adornments include glass objects from Egypt, golden coins, jewellery, filigreed ornaments of gold, silver, or enamel, precious stones and engraved scarabs. The most common weapons are bronze swords and daggers.

As in the rest of the Aegean area, the **Mycenaean period** was followed by the **geometric** and orientalizing periods (1600-650 B.C.). The excavations at Lindos, Ialyssos and Camiros brought to light an abundance of ceramic works. Painted on the Rhodian vessels of the 7th and 6th century B.C. are various animals (goats, running hares etc.), vine and date-palm leaves, even geometrical designs (rosettes, circles and swasticas). Apart from local ceramics, vases were found from Corinth, Attica, Cyprus and the Orient. The clay statuettes discovered at the Temple of Athena Lindia, at Lindos, and the Temple of Athena Polias, at Ialyssos, are of Phoenician origin.

The foundation of Rhodes in 408 B.C. made the city a pole of attraction for distinguished artists; **Lysippos** of Sikyon, the sculptor who lived at the court of Alexander the Great and made his portraits, created in Rhodes his famous four-horse chariot with the god Helios. Under the influence of Lysippos, the School of Rhodes, so much praised by Pliny, flourished for about three centuries. Among the leading artists of the School, we can mention the painter Protogenes from Karia, who, despite his talent, was very poor, until he was recognized by Apelles, and Chares of Lindos, the creator of the **Colossus of Rhodes.** There followed a number of artists, natives and immigrants, about whom little is known except their names, which often appear on the bases of the statues discovered at the **Acropolis of Lindos.** The sculptors from Chares' time onwards worked mainly in bronze. We do know a few things about Philiscos, the sculptor of a series of Muses; they were transferred to Rome most probably by

Crassus and placed in Octavia's gallery. Inspired by Lysippos, Philiscos became famous for his expertise in carving the pleats of garments; Heliodoros of Rhodes is another renowned sculptor of that era.

The loss of its independence wrought no changes as far as the artistic activities of Rhodes were concerned. The colossal statue of the 'Populus Romanus' (12m. high), which was erected at the temple of Athena Polias and Zeus Polieus, at the acropolis of Rhodes, was one of the outstanding works of art of that period. In the 2nd century B.C., the sculptor Boethos created various works destined for the sanctuary of Athena Lindia. Among originals from this century attributed to Rhodian workshops, the most noteworthy are a bronze sleeping Eros (New York, Metropolitan Museum) and the **'Victory of Samothrace'** (Louvre), one of the finest surviving pieces of Greek art. It was dedicated by the Rhodians to the sanctuary of the Cabeiroi on Samothrace, after their victory over Antiochus III (190 B.C.), and was probably created by Pythocritos, who also carved a boat in relief on the rock at Lindos; Victory is standing with her right foot on the prow of a boat which serves as the base of the statue.

The artistic school of Rhodes, from the 2nd century B.C. onwards, became one of the most important of the Hellenistic period. The **'Laocoön group'** (Vatican Museum), which was created by three Rhodian sculptors, Agesandros, Polydoros and Athenodoros, was much admired both in antiquity and during the Renaissance (it was discovered in 1506). Michelangelo

28. Laocoon (a priest of Troy) and his sons.

27. A Curved ship in relief on the rock at the entrance of the Acropolis of Lindos.

29. The statue of Wingless Victory.

refused to undertake its restoration, fearing that he would be unable to reproduce the quality of the original. Specialists believe that it was sculpted in the middle of the 2nd century B.C. That particular trend towards subjects having to do with tragedy and pathos was carried on by subsequent sculptors.

The Byzantine period offered the City of Rhodes no significant works of art or monuments; a few Byzantine fortresses and churches are all that survive of this period. The establishment of the rule of the Knights gave Rhodes the enduring character of a 15th century city. The Grand Masters, many of whom came from France or Spain, naturally favoured the style of their native country, and the French or Spanish Gothic style prevailed everywhere. The architecture of the Knights is divided into two periods; the first from 1309 to 1480 and the second from 1480 until 1522. In the beginning, the Knights employed local craftsmen to whom the Gothic style was not familiar, and as a result, their creations did not attain the technical perfection of their western models. In the second period, when Grand Master d'Aubusson (1476-1503) was governor of the city, the skill of the western architects and craftsmen who came to offer their assistance can be sensed in everything they built or repaired. The Gothic characteristic features were retained, but the form is more harmonious, the work of a higher aesthetic quality, and the décor conforms to natural or stylistic patterns. Towards the end of this second period, there appeared certain Renaissance motifs, which produced a lighter effect when mingled with the severity of the monastic Gothic style.

The walls of Rhodes, with their successive towers, are a magnificent architectural example of military fortifications of the 14th, 15th and 16th century. The inscriptions, coats of arms, and other decorative elements of the walls allow us to follow, mentally, the flow of their history. Up till the siege by the Turks in 1480, what mattered most to their constructors was their architectural form and structure. Later on, when numerous Italian engineers were employed for construction or repairs, their

30. *The Head of an Athlete. Museum of Rhodes.*
31. *The Head of Helios. Museum of Rhodes.*
32. *Grave stele dipicting Krito and Timarista: 5th century B.C.*
33. *Grave stele dipicting a dead woman, seated and a slave girl: 4th century B.C.*
38. *Plan of the City of Rhodes.*
39. *The head of a woman: 4th century B.C.*

work became more important than that of the architects of this period.

Except for a few ceramics from Anatolia, and the slightly oriental colour, an effect which was created when the prevalent Gothic style buildings and other structures blended with the tall slender minarets and fountains, the Turkish Occupation brought no significant change; as for the Italians, they did offer the island a few things, among which we can mention the rather pompous architectural style, the restorations and the extension and improvement of the road network.

The city of Rhodes

The city of Rhodes is situated at the northernmost edge of the island and has today about 32,000 permanent residents. It is divided into two sections. The walls surrounding the old city were constructed by the Knights and the whole section swings amphitheatrically around the central, or commercial port. At the northwestern part of the old city there stretches an area, enclosed in walls, which is called **'Kastello'**, and the rest of the old city is known as 'Chora'. **The Modern City** was the result of the building activity of the Italians after 1912 and of the development of tourism during the last 20 years: congested with hotels, it starts from the north of the old city and reaches the northernmost tip of the island and the foot of the ancient Acropolis towards the west, on the hill of Aghios Stefanos; it includes two quarters of the ancient city, **Marazi** and **Neochori.** On the eastern part of the Modern City is **Mandraki,** the smaller of the two harbours of Rhodes, used by only small vessels and yachts nowadays. The gardens of Rhodes are widely renowned for their oleanders, and other decorative plants. The city has been stricken by various earthquakes over the centuries: it is believed that it was the earthquake of 225 B.C. which demolished the **Colossus.** There have survived a few traces of the ancient city and archeologists have succeeded in locating the biggest part of the ancient road network under the new city.

The Modern City

The Modern City stretches along the coastline of the northern part of the island up to Mandraki, the northernmost of

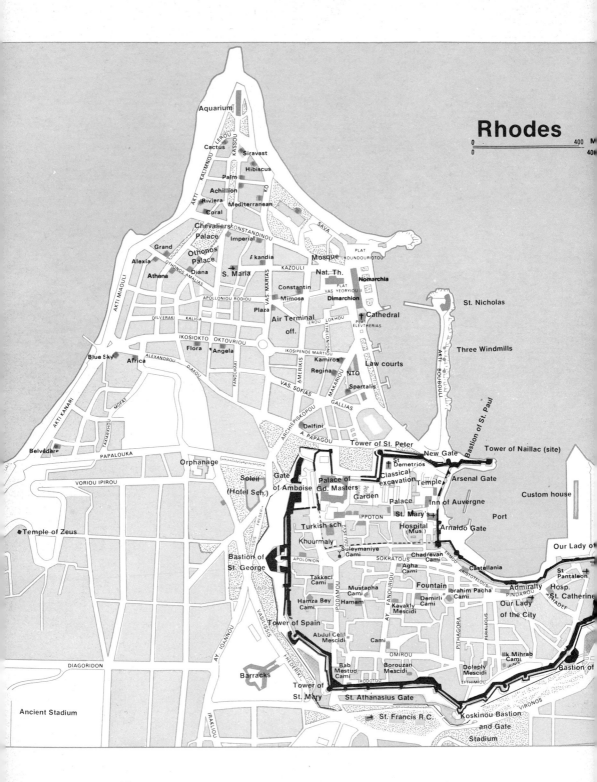

Rhodes

0   400 M
0   40

Aquarium

Cactus
Siravast
Hibiscus
Palm
Achillion
Riviera
Coral
Mediterranean
Chevaliers Konstandinou
Palace
Imperial
Grand
Othonos
Palace
Alexia
Diana
Athena
S. Maria
Fkandia
Mosque
PLAT KOUNDOURIOTOU
Nat. Th.
Nomarchia
KAZOULI
Constantin
Mimosa
Dimarchion
Plaza
Air Terminal
off.
Cathedral
St. Nicholas
Three Windmills
Flora
Angela
IKOSIPENDE MARTIOU
Kamiros
Blue Sky
Africa
Regina
NTO
Spartalis
Law courts
Delfini
A. PAPAGOU
Tower of St. Peter
Tower of Naillac (site)
Orphanage
New Gate
St. Demetrios
Soleil
(Hotel Sch.)
Gate
of Amboise
Classical
excavation
Temple
Arsenal Gate
Palace of
Gd. Masters
Garden
Palace
Inn of Auvergne
Custom house
IPPOTON
St. Mary's
Port
Temple of Zeus
Turkish sch.
Hospital
(Mus.)
Arnaldo Gate
Khourmaly
Our Lady of
Suleymaniye
Cami
Chadrevan
Cami
Castellania
St
Pantaleon
Bastion of
St. George
Agha
Cami
Admiralty
Hosp.
St. Catherine
Takkaci
Cami
Mustapha
Cami
Fountain
Ibrahim Pacha
Cami
Our Lady
of the City
Hamza Bey
Cami
Hamam
Demirli
Cami
Kavakly
Mescidi
Tower of Spain
Abdul Celil
Mescidi
Cami
Ilk Mihrab
Cami
DIAGORIDON
Barracks
Bab
Mestud
Cami
Borouzan
Mescidi
Dolaply
Mescidi
Bastion of
Tower of
St. Mary
St. Athanasius Gate
Ancient Stadium
St. Francis R.C.
Koskinou Bastion
and Gate
Stadium

44-5. *The Government House.*

its two natural harbours, equipped now for use by pleasure boats; two bronze deer mark the entrance to the city. On the mole which protects the southern part of this harbour, there stand three windmills and the **Fort of St. Nikolaos,** with a round tower that dates from 1464-67 and is equipped to serve as a lighthouse.

The name **'Mandraki',** which was given to various small closed harbours, comes from the Greek word "Mandra", or "Mandri", a small enclosure for domestic animals. Its other name, "Harbour of the Triremes", however, does not seem to have any factual basis, for Mandraki has always been of secondary importance, as compared with the commercial port; during the period of the Knights it was occupied by shipbuilders. This was probably the site of the **Colossus of Rhodes,** the bronze statue of the sun **god Helios** which was created by Chares of Lindos in 290 B.C., and is considered to have been one of the seven wonders of the ancient world. The funds to create and set it up were raised from the sale of the huge siege machines left behind by Demetrios the Besieger, after his unsuccessful siege on the city (305-304 B.C.). The head of the god Helios is said to have been ornamented with a crown, in the shape of rays emanating from it; he wore a chiton and held in his right hand a torch, which was used by sailors to help them find their bearings. The fable according to which the statue stood astride of the harbour's entrance and boats sailed underneath has no historical basis. The earthquakes that shook the city in 225 B.C. caused the colossal statue to fall and break into pieces; for eight centuries its gigantic ruins remained where they had fallen, owing to the prejudice and the piety of the Rhodians. They where finally collected by corsairs and taken to Tyre, where they were sold to Jewish merchants, who, in their turn, carried them on the backs of 900 camels, to have them melted and resell them.

The public buildings on the shore date from the Italian Occupation and they were all designed in various monumental styles by **Florestano di Fausto.** At the entrance of the harbour of Mandraki rises the square belfry of the magnificent church of **Saint John,** built in 1925 on the plans of the earlier Old-Town Gothic church of the same name, which was destroyed in 1856. Its fountain, on the west side of the church, is a 13th century reproduction of the Grand Fountain of Viterbo; the central Post Office is across the street. Near the church of Saint John, a church of the Annunciation today, is the Government House. It is the most important monument of the Italian period, a modern

47. The Palace of the Grand Master.

48. *The Mosque of Murad Reis, Admiral of the Turkish fleet.*

building with Gothic and Renaissance architectural features, which was once the Palace of the Italian Governor. Its arched, picturesque façade, ornamented with marble, which faces the sea-side of the square, blends harmoniously with the severe style of the City Hall and the Theater. Off towards the north, there is a public beach, very popular with natives and tourists, but the admission is not free.

Beyond the Theater, near the Government House, rises the tall, slender minaret of the Mosque of Murat Reis. One notices immediately the cupola that covers Murat Reis's tomb, an

49. *The Entrance to the New Agora.*   *A view of the City of Rhodes.*

admiral of Suleiman killed during the siege of 1522. At the neighbouring cemetery are buried numerous Turkish officials who had lived in exile on the island; among them are a Persian Shah and a Crimean Prince. Further off, next to the hotel of Roses (1927), the road continues towards the north on a parallel path to that of the coastline up to the Sand Cape, the northernmost tip of the island. The hydrobiological Institute there has an outstanding collection of marine animals, caught in local waters and preserved at the building. We should also mention the Aquarium, whose glass tanks house an abundance of living water animals.

The west coast of the island, lined with modern hotels, is still accessible to sea enthusiasts.

Returning southwards, through Mandraki and its gardens, on our way to the Old Town, we pass the Law Courts, a local coffee-house, and further on the Bank of Greece. Their golden-hued stone contrasts with the flat whiteness of the New Market, the large polygonal building which is the heart of the modern city. Below the northern wall of the Medieval City stretches the Garden of the Deer, in a profusion of bright tropical flowers.

The Old Town

The visitor enters the Old Town by the New Gate, or Gate of Freedom, which was opened by the Italians in 1924, and crosses Symis Square. He is now within the Kastro, the area destined for the Knights, in the part of the Medieval City which is called Kastello, and was separated from the rest of it, Chora, by an internal wall. This area includes the Palace of the **Grand Master** and the 'Lodges'. At Symis Square (or Neoriou Square), which communicates with the Commercial Port by the Gate of Neorion, there are the ruins of the **Temple of Aphrodite,** dating back to the 3rd century B.C., of which only the foundations and a few architectural members are preserved. As we cross Symis Square, with the temple of Aphrodite on our right, the first building we come to is the Lodge of the Tongue of Auvergne, a 15th century structure, repaired in 1919; one of its sides faces the lovely Argyrokastrou Square, with a fountain which was originally part of a Byzantine baptistry. To the right, there is a building that today houses the offices of the **Archaeological**

Service and the Museum Library; it was built by the Grand Master R. de Pins in the 14th century and was originally the old Hospital of the Knights. In this square we can also find the Decorative Arts Museum. Passing under an arch, we can see to our left the Panaghia of the Kastro, a Byzantine church of the 13th century, which would later become the first **Cathedral of the Order.** After 1522, the Turks converted it into a mosque, and today it is a Byzantine Museum.

In the courtyard of the building opposite, you can see an amusing modern mosaic of black and white arches, wrought in a style that has remained unchanged in Rhodian works of art from the Byzantine period onwards.

Immediately beyond Panaghia of the Kastro there is a small square in which is the main entrance to the Hospital of the Knights. Facing this square is the Lodge of the Tongue of England. It was built in 1482, was pillaged and almost destroyed in 1850, and was rebuilt on the same site and on the original plans by the British colonel Sir Vivian Gabriel; finally, in 1949, it was restored by the British.

The Hospital of the Knights, the construction of which began in 1440 on the ruins of a Roman structure and was completed in the period between the years 1481-89, is directly opposite. During the Greek Revolution in 1821, the Turks used it for their sick and wounded soldiers, but it was later turned into a barracks. In 1913-18, it was restored with much care under the direction of Amadeo Maiuri. The damages caused to its southern side by the bombs of World War II have also been repaired. The façade consists of eight arches, seven of which lead to little open-air shops, whilst the eighth, almost in the middle, supports the main entrance.

Since 1916, this building houses the Archaeological Museum. The large interior courtyard is surrounded by a double peristyle. Under the arcades one can see a few pieces of ancient art; in the middle of the courtyard there is a marble lion (1st century B.C.) and in the corners there are large numbers of stone and iron cannonballs. A staircase leads from the central courtyard to the upper floor, where there are funerary stelai and altar bases. In the middle of the E. side is the entrance to the great ward for the sick, which is divided into two aisles by a row of pointed arches. The ceiling these arches support is made of cypress wood.

The ward contained 32 beds and the patients ate on silver

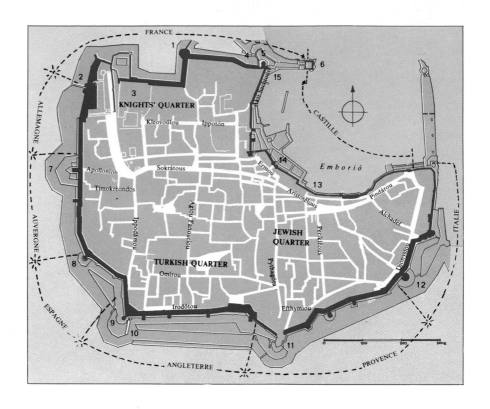

1. *Tower of St. Peter*
2. *Gate of Amboise*
3. *Palace of Gd. Masters*
4. *New Gate*
5. *Bastion of St. Paul*
6. *Tower of Naillac*
7. *Bastion of George*
8. *Tower of Spain*

9. *Tower of St. Mary*
10. *Gate of St. Athanasius*
11. *Koskinou Bastion and Gate*
12. *Bastion of Carretto*
13. *Castellania*
14. *Marine Gate*
15. *Arsenal Gate*

52. *City plan of the Old City.*

tableware. There were two surgeons on duty at all times. The dark recesses which face the ward were used as confessionals, isolation rooms, or as closets.

Under the longest wall is a vaulted platform with three Gothic windows, which advances over the main gateway. It housed an altar, where the Knights went every day to hear Mass.

53. *The entrance to the Palace of the Grand Master. Freedom Gate.*

54-5. *The Palace of the Grand Master.*
56. *A Colonnated Hall in the Palace of the Grand Master.*
    The Inner Court yard of the Palace.
57. *The Grant staircase of the Palace.*

Along the walls of the room are various gravestones belonging to Knights, which came from the destroyed church of Saint John. Also, one can see a marble sarcophagus of classic style which was used in 1355 to receive the deceased Grand Master Pierre de Corneillian and the grave stones of Thomas Newport (1502), of Nicholas de Monmirel (1511), Head of the Hospital, of Tomaso Provena (1499), and of Fernando de Xeréndia (1493). One can also observe a large number of coats of arms, including that of the royal family of England.

In the room in the south part of the ward, which was once the refectory (dining room), there is a display of reliefs, and further down, three more rooms with carvings, pieces of sculpture, etc. The visitor will immediately notice the head of the god Helios, from the sanctuary of the god in the city, the portrait of the comic poet Menander, the famous statue of the goddess Aphrodite emerging from the sea (1st century B.C.), as well as many more works of art. It is worth taking a look at the pottery dug up at the sites of Camiros and Ialyssos, at the pieces of jewellery discovered at the Mycenaean tombs of Ialyssos, and the 75 silver coins discovered at Kremaste; we should also mention the Mycenaean pottery found in Carpathos and Astypalaea, in the furthest of four more rooms.

Leaving the musuem and turning left on the square, we enter the Street of the Knights, the finest section of the Knights' city, before we reach the Palace of the Grand Masters. The buildings on it were ornamented with coats of arms that were repaired with great care during the period 1913-1916, in a way that aimed at presenting an exact picture of late medieval architecture.

The Knights' Lodges and houses are all built in the same style; they are two-storeyed, with flat ornamented façades and terraced roofs. The ground floors with the vaulted ceilings were used as storehouses or stables, and the entrance to the upper floor was through a straircase in the arcade flanking the inner courtyard. The rounded arches, the big square windows, and the rest of the decorative elements show clearly that the Renaissance had already deeply influenced the Order of the Knights of St. John, despite its entirely military character.

On our left we can now see the northern side of the Hospital and directly opposite, is the Lodge of the Tongue of

59. Vases from Ialysos.

60. *Old town near Hippocratus square.*
The square of the Jewish Martyrs.

61. Old town.
     The three windmills.

Italy, built during the period when Del Carretto was Grand Master. Further on rises the Lodge of the Tongue of France, the finest of all the Lodges, from an architectural point of view. It was built in 1492-1509, was altered by the Turks and was finally restored to its original form under the sponsorship of the French Ambassador in the Sublime Porte, as the government of the Turkish empire was officially called. The building opposite with an Aragon gate and a fine inner garden, bears the Spanish coat of arms of Villaragau. Next to it is a fine building whose upper floor is in the Turkish style.

Further along there is the small chapel of the Lodge of France, with a statue representing the Holy Virgin and Child; it also bears the emblem of the royal family of France, the fleur-de-lis. It is followed by the rectory; historians were able to date the building from the coat of arms on its facade of Grand Master Beranger, who held office from 1365 until 1374. Today it houses the Italian Consulate. A high arch bridges the street at this point: on the right is the Lodge of the Tongue of Provence, while the two building on the left are the Lodge of the Tongue of Spain.

At the end of the Street of the Knights there is a roofed open gallery which originally connected the Palace with the Church of St. John; it was already ruined before the great explosion of 1856 which destroyed the church. The old church of Saint John was built during the 14th century and was used as the burial place of the Grand Masters; after 1522 it was converted into a mosque. It was occupied later by a Turkish school.

On the north side of the square, at the end of the Street of the Knights, lies the **Palace of the Grand Masters,** which was rebuilt in the period 1939-43 according to the plans of the original 14th century building.

The Palace is built on the site of the ancient Temple of Apollo. It was started soon after the arrival of the Knights in Rhodes and was finished at the end of the 14th century. It was a magnificent edifice of rectangular shape (79×75m.), an independent fortress which was equipped with underground stores, so as to enable the Knights to hold out successfully in case they were besieged. During the periods of peace it was the official residence of the Grand Master and the place where the members of the Order met in their regular assemblies. After the earthquake of 1481, it was repaired, and did not suffer many damages during the siege of 1522 by the Turks, who converted it into a prison, when they seized the city. The earthquake of 1851 shook and damaged it badly, and the explosion of 1856 aggravated the injury it had already sustained. The Italians, wishing to make it the summer residence of Victor Emmanuel and Mussolini, restored it and made it more grandiose than the original, but their intentions never materialized, as Italy was finally forced to leave the island.

The courtyard is ornamented with Roman statues. The interior is very splendid and stately, at the expense of good taste, sometimes. The ceilings of the rooms are wooden, supported by Roman and Byzantine columns; the rooms are lined with colourful marble, or huge mosaics from Kos. The windows in some are made of alabaster. The furniture, of various styles and periods, includes fine wooden works of art from Italian Renaissance churches. From certain windows one can enjoy an enticing view of the New Market and Mandraki. In the garden there are the sarcophagi of some Grand Masters, as well as a bronze Roman shewolf, which once ornamented the eastern mole of Mandraki.

At the east side of the square, passing through a double line of arches, we arrive at Kleovoulou Square, oblong in shape and surrounded by rows of trees, interspersed by small shops and coffee-houses. On the right, an arch and a shady boulevard lead us to the Gate of Amboise; if we crossed the moats, we would find ourselves in the new city. Turning left, a short way further down we meet Chourmali Medrese, originally a Byzantine monastery later converted into a Turkish theological school.

A little further on is the mosque of Suleiman, built in 1522 on the site of the old church of the Holy Apostles; in 1808 it was re-erected on the same site and has a courtyard with a fountain, like all the other mosques. It is situated opposite the Library of Achmet Havouz, which among other centuries-old manuscripts contains an illustrated Koran of 1540. Walking down Sokratous Street, the old Bazaar, after the small Mosque of Agha, we reach Hippocratous Square, the site of the Kastellania which served as a gathering point for merchants, the office of the market inspectorate, and a merchants' court; it was built in 1507 and bears the coat of arms of Grand Master Amboise. We are now at the beginning of Aristotelous Street which heads towards the southeast part of Chora. Soon, we arrive in front of the building known as the Palace of the Admirals, overlooking the Square of

64. St. John's Gate.

the Jewish Martyrs, which lies at the entrance to the old Jewish quarter. In reality, the 'Admiralty' was a large mansion that was probably the residence of the Orthodox Metropolitan of Rhodes, or that of the Roman Catholic Archbishop, as the presence of Latin and ancient Greek inscriptions in the centre of the façade and the courtyard would seem to suggest. Continuing on Pindarou Street towards the East, the visitor comes upon the remains of the Gothic church of Sainte Marie du Bourg. This street ends at the Hospital of St. Catherine established by Fra Domenico d'Alemagna in 1392 in order to offer accommodation, initially, to the Italian pilgrims on their way to visit the Holy Land. Further on, at the northwestern edge of the Old Town, there is the small church of Aghios Fanourios, behind which, on the defence walls, rises the church of Panaghia of Victory (Ste

65. The Admiral's Gate.

66. The Gate of St. Athanasius.

Marie de la Victoire), built by Grand Master d'Aubusson after the siege of 1480 and demolished during the siege of 1522 by the troops of Suleiman the Magnificent. Nearby, on the left, is the Gate of St. Catherine, which faces the Commercial Port, the biggest of the two harbours of Rhodes (today the Gate of St. Catherine is usually called the Gate of the Mills).

This larger, commercial harbour could be closed by means of a heavy chain and was protected by the Tower of the Mills, which separated the port from Acandia Bay, and the Tower of Naillac. Traces of the moles of both the 'Great' and the 'Lesser' harbour (Mandraki) are still preserved beneath the modern moles. Following the defence walls, we can re-enter the Old Town through the Gate of Neorion, and through New Gate (or Gate of Freedom) proceed to Mandraki.

67. Amboise Gate with its cylindrical towers guarding the first bridge.

But we have not yet mentioned all the sites of the Old Town worth visiting. The tourists who have managed to find accommodation in the area of the Kastro will have many opportunities to explore the complex network of little streets leading southwards. The small houses, the picturesque churches and the mosques present a fascinating amalgam of Medieval and Oriental elements.

One of the roads leading southwards from the Admiralty area, Pericleous Street, takes us at its far end to Ilk Mihrab; rumour has it that this was the first Christian church (the church of St. George) in which Suleiman prayed after he had seized the city in 1522. Right across is Dolapli Mosque (once, probably, the church of Aghia Triada), decorated with frescoes from the 14th and 15th centuries, and towards the West, on Homirou Street,

68. *The Gateway of the Hospital of the knights (now the Archaeological museum.)*

69. *Rhodian decorative plates.*

70-1. *Statues*
of Nymphs.
72. *Roman statues of*
Dionysos (left) and
Hygia (right).
73. *Aphrodite of Rho-*
des.
74. *Part of a mosaic*
representing Tha-
leia, one of the nine
muses.
Mask of a satyr.

75. *Coins representing the Emblem of the city of Rhodes top and the head of Helios bottom.*

76. Statues in the yard of the Museum.

77. Sperveri: An Embroidered multicoloured curtain hunging above and around the bed.

there is the Mosque of Redjeb Pasha, built in 1588, the most imposing of all the Turkish buildings. Its exterior was embellished with Persian tiles, a few of which have survived.

At the centre of the Old Town, there is the Mosque of Ibrahim Pasha; this big mosque was built in 1531 and its plane-tree was used by the Turks as an execution place. Nearby we find Demirli Mosque, ruined now, which was once a Gothic church, as well as Kavakli Mestzid, a basilica with a cupola. The Mosque of Sultan Mustafa lies in a small square in a side street to the east of Hippodamou Street. It was built in 1765 and there is a Turkish Hamam (Bath) in the same square, dating from the same era. To the south of Hippodamou Street lies Takkedji Mosque; once, it also was a Greek church, that of Aghia Soteria. Finally, in the same neighbourhood, is the Abdul Tzelil Mosque, a Medieval vaulted church, which was severely damaged during World War II.

The Walls of Rhodes

The Walls of Rhodes, a masterpiece of 15th and 16th century military architecture, are preserved in good condition throughout their length of 4 kms. They successfully resisted the siege of 1480 and the longer one of 1522. They bear the coats of arms of the 151 Grand Masters who contributed to their building or modification.

In some places there are stones originally used in Byzantine or ancient foundations, but except for the fact that it held out against the Knights for three consecutive years, little else is known about the Byzantine wall. The towers are intact and some of them date back to the period before 1380, and the same applies to the moat. A reconstruction was attempted in the days of the Grand Masters **Herediat** (1377-96) and **De Naillac** (1396-1421) who built a massive tower on the northern mole of the 'Great Harbour', the present-day Commercial Port. In the period 1437-71 the walls were reconstructed so as to incorporate a number of lone-standing towers. Following the siege of 1480 and the earthquake of 1481, Pierre d'Aubusson (1476-1503) undertook a systematic and complete reconstruction; the final fortification walls were made thicker, the parapets wider and the gates more impenetrable. In addition to the fortification works, the width of the moats was doubled. The works were finished by Del Carretto (1513-21), with the assistance of Italian architects. In 1522, with Italian help again, Villier de l'Isle Adan built the final fortifications. In 1465, the perimeter of the walls was divided into 8 sections, and each Tongue of the Order was assigned a position at which it had to defend them, an arrangement that was still in force at the time of the ultimate siege (1522).

The fortifications of the Kastro included the defence wall of the mainland, the harbour wall, and the fortified moles of the harbour. There was a road (13. 7m. wide) circling the continuous steep mainland wall, protected by battlements with openings through which the soldiers were able to fire in any direction. In many positions this circular road still exists, but at a lower height. It is the second path halfway up the wall, which enabled the defenders to strike at their attackers from closer quarters. The moat around the walls is up to 45m. wide and its depth ranged between 45 and 59m.

From Kastro Square we go through the Artillery and St.

Anthony Gates and then we cross the dry moats of the Palace of the grand Masters in order to reach the wide parapet of the Gate of Amboise (1512). A three-arched bridge spans the external moat. Below our feet, among the massive round towers, is the main gate, which bears the coats of arms of the Order and the Grand Master Amboise. On top of the wall, the circuit road turns south and then passes through a second gate over an internal ditch, and through a third gate reaches a rampart which is today a shady boulevard. This rampart was exposed to enemy fire and was separated from the palace and the city by yet another moat, bridges and gates.

Continuing our way southwards, on the circular road built on the broad upper part of the wall, we leave behind us that section of it which was assigned to the Tongue of Germany, the least important defence unit, in terms of manpower. On our left, we can see Suleiman Square, the Clock Tower and Chourmali Medrese, as well as the Mosque of Suleiman. On St. George's bastion there is the coat of arms in relief of Pope Marthin V of the Order of Grand Master Antoine Fluvian (1421-37) built into the original square tower. Later a polygonal battlement was added to it and in 1496, the road that crossed it was closed down due to the construction works on the final bastion. The next section of the wall belonged to the Tongue of Tybernia, whose territory is terminated at the round Tower of Spain.

After passing the section of the Tongue of Aragon, we reach the Tower of the Panaghia (Virgin Mary), with a relief of the Virgin and Child, dating from 1441. In 1487, d'Aubusson added around the tower a large, polygonal bastion for the purpose of protecting St. Athanassios Gate; later, he closed the gate, which was opened for an exodus in 1522, was sealed again by Suleiman the Magnificent in 1531, and remained in this condition up till 1922. The wall turns eastward at that point, until it reaches Koskinou Gate, or St. John's Gate, in the territory of the Tongue of England; in this section, the difference between the old architectural style and the more recent one can be noticed very clearly. The older wall includes a tower of square shape, while the additional fortification works of 1480 took the form of a huge bastion with crescents and openings made for the use of heavier artillery.

The great Bastion Del Carretto in the region of the Fort of Italy is a combination of an older tower and a semicircular bastion from the year 1515, three stories high and 50.3 m. in diameter. As we approach the mole and the Tower of the Mills at its end, the mainland wall turns left at an angle. St. Catherine's Gate is situated exactly behind this tower. The wall now makes its way towards the Commercial Port, following the line of the seashore. Halfway along is the picturesque Marine Gate, and after a square tower with a chapel decorated with noteworthy frescoes, the Arnaldo Gate leads to the square of the Hospital. After crossing the Gate of Neorion, we reach St. Paul's Gate, from which point the wall runs along the mole on the end of which stands the Tower of Naillac. In more recent years the defence of this mole was the responsibility of the Captain of the Port.

Between St. Paul's Gate and the Gate of Amboise is the territory of the Tongue of France. It runs in an East-West direction and includes the Gate of Freedom (or New Gate) as well as St. Pierre's Tower, a round structure which bears a relief portrait of St. Pierre and the coat of arms of Pope Pius II. At St. Pierre's Tower the wall angles off towards the south, and then turns again towards the west. Following the perimeter of the Palace of Grand Masters, we arrive at our starting-point, the square of the Kastro.

The Acropolis

Walking down Ethnarchou Makariou Street, we reach the gardens where excavations brought to light a cellar containing more than 100 intact amphorae, buried under the ground probably during the 227-26 B.C. earthquake. Heading towards the hill of Aghios Stephanos (111m. high), we can easily locate a hillock called Mt. Smith, named after the English Admiral Sir Sidney Smith (1764-1840), who established an observation post there in 1802, in order to watch the movements of the French fleet. The ancient Acropolis, which was discovered in 1916 and excavated in the period 1924-29, is situated on the less steep side of the hill. On our left, among the olive groves, we can see the Stadium, which has been restored, and a small unusual theatre (the orchestra used by the chorus and 3 seats in the front row are all that are left of the original structure). A wall supports a small elevated plateau, where, on the podium of the temple of Pythian

81. Remains from the temple of Phythian Apollo, on the Acropolis of ancient Rhodes.

Apollo stand three not very graceful corner columns. Lower down there is a spring with a cistern in plaster and a watercourse connecting it with a well. The ruins of the temple of Athena Polias and Zeus Polieus stand on the northernmost point of the hill. Only a few architectural elements have survived. A winding road takes us back to the city.

Excursions on the island

Rodini

Three klm. south, on the road towards Lindos, there is a pleasant ancient park that was probably the site of Aeschines' School of Rhetoric. The park, shaded by plane-trees, has a stream running through it and peacocks strut among the little pools of water. On this site there are also the remains of a Roman aqueduct and a twenty minutes' walk brings us to the Hellenistic tomb of the Ptolemies, dug into the rock and bearing relevant ornamentation (restored in 1924).

Ialyssos and Mt. Filerimos

After a number of hotels, at the 3rd kilometer, the road leads to Malpasso. On the right of this road is the Cave of the Dragon, with a cypress at its mouth. Legend has it that a dragon was killed here by De Gauzon, a Knight of the Tongue of Provence, who later held office as a Grand Master (1346-53). The village Trianta (pop. 30,000) has a small but interesting church. A well-paved road climbs Mt. Filerimos, an isolated hill covered by evergreen trees. It is 267m. high and its uppermost part forms a plateau where once stood the ancient city of Ialyssos. The strategic importance of this hill, towering over the valley, was recognized even by the Phoenicians; in 1248, the Genoans besieged John Kantakouzenos here and it was here again that Suleiman the Magnificent established his headquarters during the final siege of 1522. All that remain of the classical acropolis are the foundations of the temple of Athena Ialyssia (of Ialyssos). Among the more recent remains we can make out the ruins of a Byzantine church. Panaghia of Filerimos, as it was once in the hands of the Knights, has a Catholic sanctuary as well as an Orthodox one; the church is impressive, despite the fact that it was restored in 1931 in an extreme way, with the addition of a new tower. Higher up stands the restored Monastery, from which point a road takes us to a ruined castle from the days of the Knights. Lower down, there is a 4th century B.C. fountain, reconstructed in 1926, and the necropolis, where 500 tombs were discovered in cemeteries of the Neo-Mycenean, Geometric, archaic, and classical periods.

3. *The road leading to the monastery of Philerimos.*
The monastery of Philerimos.

84-85. *Hot springs of Kallithea.*

Kallithea

From one of the gates in the southern section of the Walls of the Old Town, we enter the road which runs along the northeastern coast of the island. Near a large cemetery, we turn left, crossing a bridge. In a short while we can see to our right the caves of the Hellenistic and Roman necropolis (1st century B.C.-1st century A.D.). At the 10th kilometer we come to Kallithea, with its hot springs, pseudo-Moorish style buildings, and gardens, all built on the rocks of the shore. The waters of its hot springs are recommended for various complaints.

85

Lindos

It is a village of only 700 inhabitants today, but it was the most prominent of the three ancient cities, before the foundation of the City of Rhodes. During the Middle Ages it was the most important centre of the island, after Rhodes. Its beauty derives from a combination of the natural setting and the works of man built on the rock 116m. above the sea.

History: This area was inhabited by the 3rd millenium B.C. and its Acropolis dates back to at least the 10th century B.C. Emigrants from Lindos established in the 7th century B.C.

86. Acropolis of Lindos.
87. Lindos beach: The village of Lindos and Acropolis of Lindos in the background.

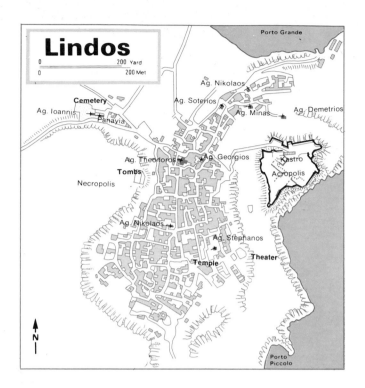

88-9. A view of the Doric stoa on the Acropolis.
91. The village of Lindos.

Parthenope (later Naples) and Zela (in Sicily). In the 6th century B.C. Lindos was governed by tyrants, amongst whom the most famous was Kleovoulos (580 B.C.), one of the Seven Sages. After the foundation of the City of Rhodes, Lindos continued to be the religious centre of the island. On his way to the City of Rhodes, St. Paul stopped there for a while. In the Byzantine period the acropolis was turned into a fortress, which the Knights of St. John used as an administration and law centre, establishing a Greek garrison and a station of twelve Knights. In 1317, Grand Master Foulke de Villaret sought refuge in the fortress, after having been removed from office by the Knights. The Turks continued to use the acropolis as a fort. From 1902 until 1952, a Danish group of archaeologists conducted excavations in the area, but the restorations were made by the Italians before 1938.

Local architecture: In Lindos there are numerous 15th century houses, in a style resembling the Gothic form used by the Knights, although the ornamentation reminds us of the

Byzantine and Turkish periods. Such houses include a residence for the housekeeper, a courtyard with an internal staircase and carved door and window posts on the main building, all done with great care. The floors are covered with mosaics made of small pieces of black and white stone. Lindian pottery adorns the interior of the houses and the ceilings are often painted in fresco.

The ceramics of Lindos: According to tradition, the Knights captured a boat carrying Persian craftsmen and held them on Lindos, where they taught the art of pottery; and certainly the Lindian plates do show an eastern influence. After the Turkish Occupation, though, the local workshops disappeared and all the plates, tiles, and other articles of pottery came from Asia Minor. The ceramics of Lindos were painted with motifs in the form of tulips, carnations, hyacinths, rosettes, etc. Since World War II, the Lindians have been producing excellent copies of this porcelain.

In the west part of the village there is a small square, shaded by mulberry-trees, with an old fountain and two restaurants. Most of the streets in the village are just wide enough for a donkey carrying a pair of baskets to pass. After the church of the Panaghia, a pathway leads up to the Acropolis.

The Acropolis of Lindos is built on the north side of a sheer cliff. From below, it looks like a huge medieval castle, an ancient fort transformed and enlarged by the Knights. On the terrace on which we stand before ascending the staircase to the acropolis, there is an exedra carved out of the rock on the left, and a relief 4,6m. long and 5,5m. high, depicting the stern of a trireme. The boat served as a base for the statue of a priest of Poseidon, named Chaleandros. On the right of this relief there are some remains of the ancient staircase (Iera Odos, sacred way). As we ascend the steep staircase to the entrance of the Castle, we can see on the left the medieval residence of the governor of the fortress. The remains of the Byzantine church of St. John inside the castle, next to the palace of the governor, are also worth mentioning.

The sanctuary of Athena Lindia takes up the major part of the area scattered with bases of statues bearing the names of local artists. After the majestic, double-winged Doric stoa, built about 208 B.C., a monumental staircase leads up to a small plateau, where there are the foundations of Propylaia, built before 407

93. Acropolis of Lindos with the remains of the temple of Athena.

94. *Reconstruction of Acropolis of Lindos by E. Dyggre.*
96. *Entrance to the Acropolis of Lindos.*

B.C. Further on is the temple of Athena Lindia, literally on the edge of the rock. The ruins date back to 348 B.C. They are above the little port surrounded by rocks where St. Paul is said to have put in. One end of the Peristyle offers a superb view of the Harbour of Lindos.

The Village. Descending the acropolis and entering the village, we pass before the residence of Phaidra Mossoridis, with a door dating from 1642. We can now leave the main road and explore a maze of streets which have retained their character through the centuries, with a multitude of old houses, courtyards and stairways.

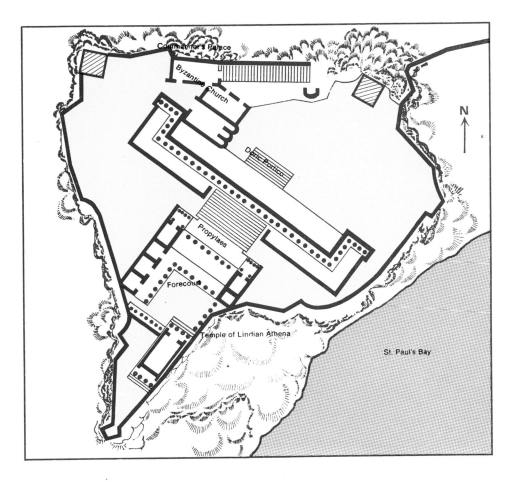

Acropolis of Lindos

Camiros

Camiros is the third of the ancient cities of Rhodes Forgotten for centuries, it was re-discovered in the excavations of 1859. The interminable ruins on the smooth slope towering above the sea remained intact during the Middle Ages. The city had neither an acropolis nor any kind of fort. The first thing to notice on arriving is a shrine dating back to the 3rd century B.C., accompanied by the insignificant traces of a Doric temple, where the main street of the city started. The excavations brought to light a number of ancient residences. In the upper part of the city is the ancient agora (market), consisting of a long row of stores,

97. Eastern part of the Doric Stoa on Acropolis.

98. *The Bell Tower of the
church of Kimissis of
Theotokou in the village
of Lindos.
The harbour of St. Paul,
south of Lindos.*

99. *A House in Lind
Doorway and windo
decorated in a typ
Village style.*

flanked by a Doric peristyle, 6 columns of which have been restored. This colonnade covered a 6th or 5th century B.C. water-tank, which was rendered useless after the invention of a new system for storing water. A little higher, among the trees, stood the temple of Athena Polias.

Modern life in Rhodes

Rhodes is indeed a fast-growing island. Apart from the city of Rhodes, which turned into a boom city when the tourist industry began flourishing, 43 towns and communities all over the island are content to share the benefits of the enormous development of tourism. The main products are wine, olive oil, tobacco, and garden produce; part of the population is still engaged in agriculture, and stock breeding (goats, sheep and

100-1. The Remains of Kamiros a village on the North of the Island.

102. The Monastery of Chambica on the Eastern Coast of Rhodes.

103. The Valley of the Butterflies.

104. *Aghios Niko-*
laos, a Byzantine
church near the
village at Foun-
dukli.

105. *Top: The inte-*
rior of the By-
zantine church of
the monastery of
Thari in the vil-
lage of Laerna.
Bottom: The In-
terior of the
church of Evan-
gelistria in the
city of Rhodes.

106. Detail from the fresco of the Archangel Michael.

cattle) is a profitable occupation, as one third of the terrain is pasture-land, while another third is covered by forests.

After the siege of 1522 by the Turks and the capture of the city, the Greek population was driven outside the walls. The Rhodians managed to survive, though, and have extended the city's territory in the last 50 years. The Italians erected magnificent structures (the New Market, the Law Courts, the Post Office, the Government House, the Port Authority Building etc.), which transformed the city, giving it a striking appearance, with its mixture of architectural styles.

On leaving the island, the visitor to Rhodes takes with him the feeling that in this setting of sunshine and emerald-green waters he has caught a glimpse of an age-old civilization, which, from mainland Greece up to Asia Minor, Cyprus and Near East, blends antiquity and the modern world into an unforgettable unity of space and time.

108. Handmade Cera-
mics and Carpets.

110. A gift shop.

111. *Typical Rhodian Houses.*

112. The reconstructed Theatre on the Acropolis of Rhodes.